I0409041

# THE MONEY BAG SALESMAN

A Salesman whose turn over resonates world over

**BY**

**LEGEND IRA**

**The money bag Salesman**

# Table of content

# Book Review

Every organization or field of sales has a standout salesman who stands out from the pack. Not only are his results great, but it appears like everyone on the team wants this individual to succeed, including the boss, subordinates, the marketing team, the support team, the administrative team, and even the janitor! "The Money Bag Salesman" is a detailed examination of such salespeople's qualities and attributes, as well as the secrets underlying their success. The gap between normal salesmen and "The Money Bag Salesman" is startling; an average salesperson hits his quota target—most of the time—while "The Money Bag Salesman" not only hits targets regularly but also has blow-out months and quotas. He earns the respect, loyalty, and referrals of his prospects. The "money bag Salesman" has more to give clients than simply just an exciting pitch—he's an enthusiastic guy with resilience who takes the time to get to know his customers' requirements by making the customer "family," demonstrates empathy, and is always sensitive to communicate sufficiently and effectively. He manages rejection and setbacks calmly, and he always learns from both his successful and unsuccessful agreements. "The Money Bag Salesman" did not become a "rockstar" overnight; success in sales requires a lot of time, work, and continuous growth. All purchasing decisions are influenced by emotions. We all experience these feelings from time to time. These feelings are natural and acceptable. The crucial issue is to consider how your product or service can address these fundamental emotional demands, as emotions skew assessments. When you successfully appeal to this basic feeling, you may elicit such strong buying desire that pricing becomes secondary, if not irrelevant. This book emphasizes the need for a Salesperson to develop a powerful relationship-the "family" like link between him and his clients. Nothing stimulates the customer's appeal of patronage more than his emotions, and nothing else works on your customer's emotions as well as you having a "family" like relationship in place. LEGEND IRA took great effort to ensure that your needs and questions as a Salesperson are effectively reflected in this masterpiece: "THE MONEY BAG SALESMAN."

# Introduction

Working in sales isn't simple, as every Salesperson knows, even if you enjoy selling. Even the most seasoned salesmen feel the strain of working in such a competitive and saturated market, which is why, as a sales professional, you need a set of practices you can rely on to keep you feeling calm, focused, and ready to take on your next challenge. If your sales self-care arsenal is lacking, affirmations are a fantastic place to start. Affirmations are positive remarks that are meant to be encouraging, inspiring, and supporting. According to academic studies, repeated affirmations can help people retain positive self-esteem, reduce defensiveness, and overcome perceived challenges to competence. That sounds like an excellent resource for salesmen who need to maintain their confidence while dealing with rejection and uncertainty.

A salesperson must convert products and services into money and, in rare situations, other valuable objects to raise or increase their company's earnings. "The Money Bag Salesman" is the instrument a salesperson needs to reinforce past results and ensure future outcomes. The book is a helpful friend to any Salesperson who is struggling and considering quitting because of his inability to meet targets and achieve great sales feats; the book is also a motivator for those who are already successful in Sales; and Companies and Organizations can find this book useful in managing Sales staffs. An average Salesperson faces a slew of obstacles daily that must be overcome to create opportunities. "The money bag Salesman" will be attempting to bring home ideas and action points that, if followed, will force the chief executive of your company to call you on the field and say, "Weldone, your figures turn over are positive.

# Key idea 1

# A NO! is a YES! whose time hasn`t come.

It's always no until it's yes.

When your success necessitates asking others for commitments, you may expect to hear no just as many—if not more—than yes. It's the nature of the business we call selling, and no one, no matter how adept, is immune. It is critical to understand that the word "no" just means "not right now," and that you have not been personally rejected. It's always a "no" until it's a "yes." No businessperson wakes up every morning anticipating that a salesman will contact them to set up a meeting. They are not enthused about the possibility of devoting their time to a salesperson who may waste it; time wasted cannot be regained. A person will refuse your meeting for only one reason: they feel it will be a waste of their time. They may also say "No" to meeting with you because they already have a partner who they think is meeting their requirements, or because they don't have the time or energy to trade another salesman whose flaws they've learned to deal with; for another who may be even worse. Even if you have something of actual worth to offer in exchange for a meeting, such as a hypothesis on why they should change some aspects of their services and how to better outcomes accessible to them, you will still be told "no." The "no" you hear now is not permanent. It could be for today, and perhaps tomorrow. The no spans a period that, however lengthy it is, is likely to be shorter than you assume.

A contract where money isn't an issue is the rarest of all unicorns in the world of sales. Money has always been and will continue to be an issue. Many of the organizations you contact will decline larger and better investments, preferring to assume that there is some competitor somewhere who can provide them with better, faster, and cheaper service. When you give them the red pill, which would open their eyes to the truth that the better outcomes they desire would cost them a larger investment, they decline, opting instead for the blue pill and continuing to live with their unsatisfactory results until you overtime justify the necessity for the red pill and address their worries. A salesperson  is caring enough to provide value for the client, which often includes assisting them in changing their thoughts. When your desired customer says yes to your rival, you are left with a no, a loss if you will. No one is immune to this fact;

you may do everything correctly and yet lose, or you can do everything incorrectly and still win. It's also possible that your services and products fell short of expectations, or, excuse me for stating this, that you didn't place it well. Your ideal client may have met your competition, or your competitor may have simply outsold you. Many salespeople consider a loss as permanent when in real sense it is everything but; simply a no now, not forever. I recently heard about a salesman who lost an account because the client believed they were failing as a firm, the client believed inflated promises from a rival who overtime couldn't deliver, only to later learn how wonderful this salesperson's company was. Guess who is returning home?

The nature of no is that it does not last forever. Situations change. Needs too change over time. Context alters preferences. People may say no to you today out of poor decision-making. The nature of no in sales is that, it's volatile. It is inclined to changing at any given hour.

The mistake you may make in sales is believing that the no you are hearing now covers a longer period than it is capable of covering. It is much shorter than you think. People who say they will never work with you will eventually renege. People will assure you they will never change relationships, only to change partners a few months later.

Forever is far longer than you imagine. And it is far less time than your client believes.

You may reprogram your subconscious mind, improve your communication skills, create and achieve objectives, and overcome sales' "NO" with perseverance and positivity by incorporating affirmations into your daily practice. Remember that sales success begins with a cheerful mindset. One of the most challenging things for inexperienced salespeople to do is convert the first "no" into a "yes." Many new salespeople avoid openly asking prospects for business until they get over the hump for fear of rejection. Many salesmen despise hearing the word "no." To them, it represents failure, rejection, and squandered time — all of which we connect with pessimism, a stagnating job, and (maybe most crucially) a little commission check.

But "no" does not have to be a frightening word. Indeed, a well-known sales adage goes, "Every no I hear brings me closer to a yes." This is fundamentally correct. The more people you talk to, the more likely one of them will purchase; so, moving on to someone new will get you one step closer to a yes – a terrific motivator to get back up and keep going.

**Here is how to turn a "no" into a "yes." In sales.**

**Your "yes" questions should be rephrased into "no" questions.**
Making further cold calls isn't the only approach to change a "no" into a "yes." One method to utilize no to your advantage is to give prospects control. After all, it's simpler to say no than yes. You can, for example, ask particular questions where no is truly excellent news, such as "Would you oppose X?" No?

Great!" By rebranding the question, you're transforming a "no" into a "yes," which can create an avenue for a "yes" sometime in the future.

## Use "nos" to build Relationships

Another approach to look at "no" is as a chance for prospects to relax their guard and open out to you. You'll never receive a yes if your prospects hang up inside the first seven seconds. Strangers are skeptical of salespeople, but if you dare to ask for a "no" instead of a "yes," you'll be communicating directly, rather than relying on manners or niceties in your discussions, which can be counterproductive if people are hesitant to tell you how they truly feel. This not only buys you more time with the prospect, but it also buys you more trust since they know you will not bully them into saying a yes.

## Rephrase their response

This is known as mirroring in sales. Prospects may not always mean what they say; they may simply be attempting to get out of the conversation. By repeating the previous few things they spoke, you demonstrate that you're paying attention and asking for clarification in their language. By this, you are making them aware that their refusal may be out of place. You'll be shocked at how successful mirroring may be, especially if you can stay quiet while the possibility opens up. Pay close attention to what they're saying if this happens. They'll almost certainly tell you all you need to know.

## To find the true objection, ask follow-up questions.

No does not imply never. Turning a "no" into a "yes" ultimately boils down to recognizing the prospect's true issue and responding professionally and pleasantly. A "no" shouldn't be the end of the road. When you hear that, attempt to figure out why the prospect is feeling that way so you can provide a solution. Perhaps the time is incorrect, or (hopefully) they misunderstood some component of your goods. In any event, delving further into a "no" can assist in steering you in the right direction, like a road map to a sale.

Inquire about what would be required for the transaction to be a success for them. "What's holding you back?" Inquiring can make the client talk and assist you ascertain what's amiss, if at all, might return them back on board.

## Remove yourself from the outcome.

Salespeople must become accustomed to hearing "no." It will no longer have the capacity to knock us back on our heels once it seems like part of the work, and we will no longer have to spend hours or days feeling down in the dumps or discouraged over getting turned down. It's similar to exercising in that it aches at first and leaves you feeling awful. However, after a while, you adjust and even begin to embrace the agony - here is where true growth occurs.

Your attitude to hearing "no" will once again influence whether or not you can transform it into a yes. Don't become irritated, don't dispute the possibility, select your words wisely, and always keep a cheerful attitude. And, if you can't get over the "no," don't be scared to go on to the next door step. There are several opportunities available, and the phrase we mentioned previously is accurate. No can help you get closer to yes. Never be frightened to hear the word "no," since it is the one word that all salesmen must become accustomed to if they are to prosper.

## Sales Pitch

It appears like I am hearing it more frequently. Or do I hear it more frequently because I pay attention to it? 'When the buyer says 'no,' the selling begins." This has been a popular catchphrase among self-proclaimed sales specialists, who have done significant harm to clients' confidence. You've undoubtedly received a sales call from someone trying to sell you a membership. I'm sure you've been approached by a representative from an energy provider or a lottery. It happens to me all the time. We come across salespeople regularly who act like bugs and simply refuse to let us be. Yes, they! The NO | NO motion or wave you make up, which is primarily designed to keep their unsolicited advertising pamphlets out, appears to be an invitation to annoy you with additional unsolicited sales pitches. As though they think: ' If you don't want to buy something from me the calm approach way, then we go the forceful method because the selling process begins when the consumer says "no." When I tell them I'm not interested, it tends to energize them and keep them going. They appear to be aware that they will occasionally capture something. Furthermore, sales trainers tell these young men and women that selling begins when the buyer says "no." That sounds fantastic. And so it goes on. Because "selling" begins when a consumer says "no." Every time I hear this, I see myself giving my kid this advise shortly before his first date: "Kid, don't forget: it all starts when she says 'no.'" Customers will continue to say 'no' to you if you follow this rude mindset. This kind of selling reinforces their dislike of invasive sellers, or that they will eventually say 'yes' when they do not want to buy from you at all. It will be the seller's sausage since his aim has been met and his commission has most likely been earned. However, selling to consumers who aren't seeking you, haven't asked for you, and who say 'no' in the first place assures both short-term success and long-term damage. It is known as opportunism.

## How to Attract New Customers

"How can I gain new clients when I'm supposed to accept "no" as part of the job?" the salesperson asks, a little dramatically. You may boost your sales by doing the following:

Understanding who your consumers are and what they require.

Knowing their location

Being noticeable

Being able to track

Being pertinent

Being appealing

Being approachable

The aforementioned suggestions may bring you to clients seeking you or a service like yours. They are the clients who will gladly say 'yes' to you because you enable them to, not because they have to. Not for your benefit, but for the benefit of their needs.

**When the consumer replies 'yes,' the selling process begins.**

Once you have such a customer, it is critical to service, maintain, and develop the customer properly by digging into the customer, paying attention to him, listening, and delivering your services appropriately. By assisting and providing the most pertinent advice. By providing relevant solutions and providing unique consumer experiences. Ensure from a website visit to a quote request, purchase, after-sales service, and maintenance, the customer is well serviced. When the customer replies 'yes,' the selling process begins.

## Key idea 2

# Embody and Exhume Humor when needed

**Humor cuts through the clutter;** if you can get your prospect laugh fast, you'll be a ray of sunshine in their day. When humor is brought into a discussion at a time when the receiver least anticipates, it generates an incongruity, striking them by surprise as it is 'unexpected'. As a result, in order to transmit messages throughout the selling process, a salesperson must recognize and manifest linguistic indicators that are contradictory with consumers' normal expectations for the conversation. Instead of arguing with your prospect, concede to him with humor and pitch immediately; for example, if you are unable to agree on whether the warranty duration span on a product is adequate, you could say something like: "I know you are a Hulk fan" Do you think we really need an additional warranty clause?" Ideally, the prospect would have expected you to debate, but his expression violated an accepted social standard. Nonetheless, being a Hulk fan, the prospect regarded the message as harmless owing to the descriptive sense of the language.

When a violation and a benign event occur at the same moment, the prospect will capitulate and begin smiling. As a result, you have effectively crafted a humorous message that is a harmless transgression of a societal norm. Laughter, on a biological level, produces endorphins, making us feel pleased and so forming a link between individuals. As a result, if you can successfully include or employ humor into your "sales game," prospects will link sentiments of optimism with you and your offer.

**What makes a joke amusing?**

**Surprise** - This is an essential component of each joke. A strong punchline, like the Incongruity-Resolution Theory, can violate certain assumptions your prospect may have formed in his brain, catching them off guard and forcing them to chuckle.

**Authenticity** - Regardless matter what you're discussing, authenticity is essential for connecting with others. When telling jokes, be sincere since people want to know you understand what they're going through.

**Relatability** - Making a joke about the industry's typical pain points will undoubtedly warm your prospects' hearts - after all, these are situations we can all relate to. The challenge is to portray those common experiences in a palatable and accessible manner.

## Caution

**Understand your target audience** - A salesman made a millennial joke in front of a group of HR officials. Unfortunately, one of those execs was a mature-looking millennial who thought the joke was inappropriate. The salesperson was never given another chance. So you may have a great joke ready to tell to every customer you encounter. But hold your horses! Consider your audience and tailor your jokes to the recipient(s).

**Limit your use of sarcasm** - Some individuals adore sarcasm, while others despise it. It is best to use it with caution and sparingly. You can try it once, and if it fails, you can stop trying to be sarcastic in the future.

**Avoid making contentious jokes** - Of course, there are certain obvious no-nos: Politics, religion, athletics, and even climate change are all on the table. If you're unsure whether a subject is acceptable, leave it out. Instead, utilize a joke that is always safe and cannot be punished: your own!

## Various approaches of using humour into sales

Now that you understand the fundamentals of using humor in sales, you may be asking how to truly make your consumers laugh because you appear to lack such a bone. Well, humor doesn't always have to be in the form of spontaneous one-liners, because not everyone is a comic with a monologue. Here are some methods you may boost your confidence and obtain the correct joke elements to infuse into your sales interactions:

- Watch a lot of humor performances
- Make use of humorous formulae.
- Comic Triple
- Triple reverse

Humans are 70-90% emotional and 20-30% rational, according to research. However, whether you believe it or not, we humans are a complex collection of emotions.People buy with their emotions and rationalize their purchases with rationality. I'd like you to look at any things or products you've lately purchased and ask yourself why you got them in the first place; you may offer a rational justification. However, if you examine closely and peel back the layers, you'll see that these are your emotions getting the best of you. Keeping this in mind, it's critical for salespeople who want to hit the bag to tap into this and stock his humour arsenal before the day of use.

**Key idea 3**

# Customers are "Family".

Happy customers may become advocates for your product or service, spreading the word and bringing in new business, with good customer relationship management. A delighted consumer is already persuaded to become a brand ambassador for your company. When it comes to customer service, aim for utter happiness rather than contentment. By delighting your customers, you may transform them into great salespeople who encourage friends, family, and colleagues to utilize your products and services. Exceeding your customer's expectations may be a big differentiator between you and your competition. It should improve your reputation and income, as well as assist you to focus your sales efforts because satisfied customers are considerably more likely to persuade others to buy from you. Simply put, they serve as the front line of your sales team. Customer evangelists are not created by chance; it begins with amazing, customer-focused service and a dedication to customer retention, and to keep a client, you must make him feel more like a "family." Customer retention is critical. According to research, selling to existing clients is five times simpler than selling to new ones. You need a company strategy that prioritizes keeping existing customers while seeking new ones. However, maintaining customers may be difficult because every customer is important. If you're a small business with a few high-value clients and aren't properly servicing them, you risk losing them. It is quite simple to change vendors. What will keep your existing clients from leaving if you don't nurture them?"

Customer retention often results in repeat sales. What underpins excellent services is knowledge. It is critical to become closer to your consumers. You must maintain your finger on the pulse of what they are doing. You need to know when they last bought from you when their contract is up for renewal, and who the biggest spenders are. You should probably have a solid sense of what your consumers' demands are and when they are likely to buy from you. However, the more consumers you have, the more information you must keep track of.

Maintaining accurate records, whether using Excel, Google spreadsheets, or a customer relationship management (CRM) system, should allow you and your team to keep track of your clients. If you need to keep track of more than a few clients and potential customers, or if you need to exchange information with staff across the company, specialist CRM software is generally the best solution. Aside from making it simple to record what you know, the finest CRM software may include features to help you better understand your customers, find new prospects, and automate marketing mailshots, among other things. A good CRM system is the cornerstone of every successful salesman. You just cannot remember everything when you have so many diverse ties - with suppliers, clients, and prospects. Ideally, you should keep track of all of your phone conversations, meeting notes, emails, and decisions.

You have remarkable visibility with excellent CRM software since you can see exactly what's going on and what your competitors are doing. It also allows you to rank your prospects from warm to hot and provide relevant, real-time data, allowing you to quickly identify where the sales possibilities are.

## How to Get Customer Referrals

A gentle nudge may be worth its weight in gold since it reassures the customer that you respect their feedback even after the deal has been completed. Furthermore, providing a simple incentive such as a discount on their next purchase might motivate consumers to share their comments and refer you to others. Always express gratitude for good referrals and reply gracefully to all online evaluations, whether positive or negative. Following up after each transaction is important to gain firsthand feedback on what you did right - and wrong. If there were any issues with the customer experience, address them as soon as possible and properly to reduce the likelihood of a negative review surfacing online. Salespeople are useful, but nothing matches a suggestion from a third party. Having your clients sell for you is powerful, and it provides more credibility than any salesperson.

## Be Proactive

When I ask my clients and consumers what the most valuable attributes a salesman may have, they frequently cite a proactive attitude. This applies to any department inside the salesperson's organization that services the customer, from customer support to billing. When things go wrong, it's the perfect chance to demonstrate to them that what you promised in the first place is what they'll get. When an issue is quickly resolved, it is easier to create trust than when there are no difficulties at all. And trust isn't always formed by solving issues; it may be as simple as answering a question. Each consumer wants to feel like they are the most important person on your list like they are part of a family.

## Empathic

Connecting with your consumers' emotions might reveal what they truly desire from a deal. You may address their wants in novel ways by appealing to their emotions. Consider yourself in your consumers' shoes and the issues they confront. By showing real care for your client's needs — and effectively resolving them — you demonstrate that you are truly devoted to their best interests rather than merely attempting to make a sale. This was taught to me through experience, If you are not prepared to take care of your clients, I guarantee that someone else will. Getting a sale is similar to entering into a relationship. Let me explain in more detail: Starting with the first date, then following up, proposing to them, and making them feel important enough to remain with you forever, sounds more like a family. Consider how you met your girl on your first date. You will put on your finest clothing. You will arrive on time. You will also conduct a thorough examination of her Facebook and Instagram accounts. So you have enough material to discuss with her. The same is true for your initial sales meeting. You must look your best and wear your best attire. You must always arrive ahead of schedule. You must do a consumer analysis. What exactly are their issues? How will your product address their concerns? On their first date, desperate individuals make the mistake of chatting too much. The genuine date should be all about having a good time. It only happens when both parties participate. The same may be said for your sales meeting. Create a fantastic discussion by enabling them to open up, understanding their needs and challenges, and telling them how your solution solves the problem and relieves their suffering.

Asking your consumer for the final contract on the first date is analogous to asking a lady to marry you on the first date. Yes, we are desperate singles, but trust me when I say that creating interest in her through numerous outings would work better. The same is true for your client's, regular visits to discuss his project, his family, your family, and your connection. When the moment comes, inject your product to seal the deal.

## Follow-up

In relationship you have to work hard to attract your partner, be attentive, take them out, compliment them, give them things, spend all of your time with them, and so on. However, if you become too comfortable and stop paying attention to them, another guy will begin to pay attention and do all of the things you aren't doing, and she may finally leave you. Allowing another guy to make his ladies smile is a man's worst mistake. The same idea applies to the sales process; if you do not follow them, someone else will.

**The money bag Salesman**

Women appreciate surprises, so bring some with you when you meet. In sales, surprise customers with product characteristics that set you apart from the competition. Customers want someone they can rely on, and that person may be you.

Key idea 4

# Your words and actions are your genuine identity

Consumers are considerably more inclined to purchase from someone with whom they can relate - someone who appears real and trustworthy. Building rapport is made simpler by just being yourself and leading with honesty. And, as every good salesperson knows, creating a relationship is frequently the difference between a yes and a no. When defining a company and sales plan, an essential decision must be made: to suppress information or to be completely upfront with the facts. And, yes, there are dishonest salesmen out there, but here's the finest sales advice you'll ever get: don't be one of them! Those who continuously choose truth over deceit are the most effective salesmen. They prefer to under-promise and over-deliver rather than exaggerate during a sales meeting. Instead of withholding difficult truths, they aggressively disclose all pertinent information to their clients. Top sales professionals understand that honesty in sales is arguably the most successful long-term success technique. The good news for salesmen is that honesty is not just the best moral policy but the most important. Sincere communication is also a profitable sales tactic that can help you advance in your job. Remember that confidence does not imply being forceful or unduly demanding. To develop trust with consumers, you must have the perfect mix of expertise, preparedness, honesty, and empathy. We all know that pleased consumers become loyal customers, but did you realize that imply being honest creates leads? Customers who have a pleasant experience are not only more likely to buy from you again in the future, but they will also send you referrals of their friends, relatives, and neighbors. Sincerity fosters self-confidence; once you understand you don't need to rely on white lies, exaggerations, and "tricks of the trade" to make a sale, you'll become a more confident seller. Not only will you sleep easier at night knowing that you did business with integrity, but this increase in self-esteem will make you a better seller and team leader. Never be scared to tell the truth for fear of scaring off a possible purchase. Remember that a strong salesman is distinguished by both the number and quality of sales. Concentrate on being completely honest, truthful, and real. Not only is this the proper thing to do, but it may also put you on the fast road to attaining your professional objectives. The advantages of honesty in sales conversations cannot be overstated. Everyone has heard the adage, "Honesty is the best policy." The problem is that saying became a cliché because it's true. And this one is right down to the bone.

**Reasons to be brutally honest in sales talks**

The truth is simpler to remember than all of your lies together. If you have to employ deception to get a piece of business, there is something seriously wrong with either the buyer or the seller.

What you want is the customer's honesty, and they want it from you as well.

Honesty minimizes the need for guessing games.

If you demand honesty, you must provide it.

Long-term partnerships need honesty. Honesty is the roadway to the best-fitting consumers. Being brutally honest screens out non-ideal consumers and attracts those who are a good fit. The sooner you recognize that an opportunity isn't great, the sooner you can devote your time and efforts to the appropriate opportunity. The greatest way to get there is to be honest.

Demand now outnumbers supply in nearly all sales sectors, making it a seller's market. It's a seller's market, and you're in command. In a seller's market, you may be a little more daring than in the past; there's no better place to test out some harsh honesty. Because clients have fewer alternatives right now, you can be confident that losing business will be considerably more difficult. If you're afraid of expressing the truth and losing business in this market, that tells me you need to lose it. When you discover the true value of honesty, your fear of being honest will go – quickly. Sometimes, after conversing with all partners in your company's decision-making chain, a salesperson might grasp a buyer's needs better than they do initially. Great salespeople utilize this knowledge to walk their consumers through the benefits and drawbacks of each competitor's product. Competitors may misrepresent their products, and it is the job of excellent

Salesmen to function as consultants in the best interests of the customer. Lying may be harmful to both the consumer and the vendor. If the product or service fails to function properly after being paid for, the consumer may terminate the service or return the merchandise. They may even go so far as to sue the seller for monetary damages or harm the merchant's reputation through unfavorable reviews. Contracts are quite vital in these situations; contract writing should essentially begin with the first conversation and go throughout the selling process.

**Key idea 5**

# Avoid ambiguities when Communicating with clients.

Ambiguity can cause uncertainty and misconceptions, as well as being misinterpreted as dishonest, which can be damaging to a sales call. A potential consumer may be hesitant to purchase if they are unsure about the product or service supplied. Similarly, if the selling conditions are unclear, the consumer may be hesitant to commit to the transaction. Communication is the glue that holds the connection together, whether it's before, during, or long after the sale. Make it easier to communicate by stating things like, "Let me see if I understand what you're saying," or "Just to make sure we're on the right track, are these the three concerns you're concerned about?" This will assist in the elimination of ambiguity.

## The money bag Salesman

When individuals truly listen, good communication occurs. It's also a good idea to ask your clients how often they want to be contacted following the transaction. Once a week? Every month? Every customer is unique. When interviewing, I usually ask, "Is there anything the firm or salesperson isn't doing that they should be doing to better serve you?" This inquiry normally unveils needed information from the customer, which may help you manage his account effectively and prevent little issues from becoming major ones. A skilled salesperson should be an expert in the product or service they are selling. You wouldn't buy a car from someone who couldn't tell you anything about its mileage or safety features in plain English, would you? Customers will see you as more credible if you can demonstrate your knowledge. Being thorough allows you to detect and address possible problems or objections early on. Customers like thoroughness because it demonstrates expertise, dependability, and a dedication to providing outstanding service. Ambiguity in sales talks can be fatal to a deal. You may lose prospects if you do not provide them with a clear grasp of what they are purchasing. This detailed book will teach you why and how to effectively avoid ambiguity in sales conversations.

## What is Ambiguity?

Communication is essential in the sales industry. To minimize misconceptions, it is critical to use precise and simple language while speaking with potential consumers. This is when ambiguity enters the picture. Ambiguity in communication refers to a lack of clarity or accuracy. It might happen when a person is confused about what someone is attempting to communicate or when there are various interpretations of a message. Ambiguity can cause uncertainty and misconceptions, which can harm a sales call. A potential consumer may be hesitant to purchase if they are unsure about the product or service supplied. Similarly, if the selling conditions are unclear, the consumer may be hesitant to commit to the transaction. In both scenerio ambiguity can lead to losing sales.

## Types of Ambiguities Sales Call

Sales calls are critical in converting potential consumers into loyal customers. However, uncertainty in these exchanges can stymie the process and result in misunderstandings or missed opportunities. In this section, we will look at numerous sorts of ambiguity in a sales call, such as purposeful ambiguity, unintentional ambiguity with a unclear pitch, and strategic ambiguity.

## Unintentional Ambiguity with unclear Pitch

Unintentional ambiguity happens when a salesman unintentionally causes misunderstanding or misinterpretation by using the wrong words or explanations. This form of ambiguity can be caused by a variety of circumstances, including:

- Using jargon or technical terminology that the customer may not be familiar with.
- Inadequate product or service information, leaving the customer with unresolved questions.
- Failure to meet the customer's requirements or concerns, confusing the product's or service's acceptability.
- Communication breakdowns, which are caused by language hurdles or bad phone connections.

## Strategic Ambiguity

Strategic ambiguity is an intentional approach used by salespeople to generate interest or curiosity in their product or service. This method can be used to:

- Encourage the consumer to ask additional questions, which will allow the salesperson to engage in a more in-depth dialogue and uncover the customer's demands.
- Instill a sense of exclusivity or scarcity in your consumers, making them feel forced to act swiftly lest they lose out on a once-in-a-lifetime chance.
- Allow the salesperson to modify their pitch based on the reactions of the customers, allowing them to tweak their message for optimum effect.

Strategic ambiguity should be utilized with caution, since it might backfire if the consumer feels dissatisfied or confused due to a lack of clear information. It is critical to find a balance between piquing the customer's interest and offering enough information for them to make an informed decision.

Understanding the different sorts of ambiguity in sales calls is critical for minimizing unintended misunderstanding and maximizing the potential of purposeful ambiguity. Salespeople may successfully express their message and boost their chances of completing deals and developing long-term client connections by being aware of these possible hazards and using clear, succinct communication.

**Ambiguity in brand communication** occurs when messaging is inconsistent across numerous commercials, promotions, and social media channels. This can be caused by a disconnected narrative, a lack of a consistent brand concept, or different perceptions of the brand's identity. When various messages are delivered across several channels, clients and potential consumers become confused, making it harder for them to comprehend the genuine core of the business. Inconsistency can be caused by a lack of cooperation among marketing departments, imprecise branding rules, or frequent brand plan revisions. As a result, ambiguity impedes the development of a strong brand identity and makes it difficult for customers to generate trust and loyalty to the company. To eliminate ambiguity in brand communication, a clear and consistent brand story that connects with the target audience across all marketing channels must be established. Businesses may build a closer relationship with their consumers in this way, resulting in enhanced brand awareness, customer loyalty, and long-term success.

## Intentional Ambiguity in Your Pitch

To make a purchase look more appealing and presumably a no-brainer for the buyer, salespeople may sometimes purposely conceal specific features of their products or solutions. While this method may appear to be profitable in the near term, it is neither sustainable nor ethical. The ideals of integrity and honesty, which are vital for creating confidence and credibility in any business partnership, are violated by concealing facts. Furthermore, when clients learn the hidden facts, they will likely feel tricked and betrayed, leading to a loss of confidence and maybe permanently breaking relations with the organization.

In the long term, such activities can harm a company's reputation and make it difficult to acquire and keep loyal customers. To create long-term customer relationships, sales professionals must stress honesty and open communication. Effective sales techniques need clear and straightforward communication. While uncertainty might be important in building intrigues at times.

Transparency and honesty are essential in every business connection for building trust and confidence. Salespeople should stress open communication and avoid dishonest methods that might affect their reputation and hamper their ability to recruit and maintain loyal customers. Salespeople may successfully deliver their message and boost their chances of completing agreements and developing long-term client connections by stressing honesty and straightforward communication.

## Avoiding Ambiguity

To minimize ambiguity in sales calls, it is critical to use clear and exact wording. The following are some considerations to make during a sales call, brand communication, or other form of promotional activity:

- Use basic wording that the customer can comprehend.
- Use of unfamiliar or technical terms should be completely avoided..
- Use ordinary terminology that the customer is comfortable with.
- Give specifics on the characteristics and benefits of the product or service.

- Explain how the product or service will suit the demands of the consumer.
- To demonstrate points, use examples and tales.
- Be open and honest about price and delivery alternatives.
- Explain any additional pertinent information in detail.
- Ascertain that the consumer understands and agrees to what they are receiving.
- To minimize misunderstanding, keep your brand communication consistent across all social networks.

In conclusion, minimizing uncertainty during sales calls is crucial to closing agreements and developing great customer relationships. You can guarantee that potential buyers understand the product or service and the conditions of sale by using clear and precise wording. This can result in greater sales, happier consumers, and a better reputation for your company.

**Key idea 6**

# Be sensitive and always pay keen attention to body language

While understanding what to do in meetings and negotiations is vital, knowing what not to do is frequently just as important - and it starts with lousy body language.

The finest sales managers understand that even if you have a flawless sales presentation, stylish dress, and a product that virtually sells itself, you may still lose a sale if your body language does not match your words. While initial impressions are essential, cumulative body language is also significant. If you have a history of using negative body language in sales meetings, it might be enough to harm your sales effectiveness and turn a possible yes into a definite no.

**Things to Avoid**

**Crossing your arms** conveys apathy and lack of confidence. Crossing your arms, unless done to make a clear point, simply serves to disrupt the flow of a constructive conversation.

**A week handshake** A feeble handshake conveys little excitement and also implies a lack of confidence. A weak handshake, whether icy and boney or warm and squishy, is unnerving and should be avoided.

**An overly firm handshake** on the other hand, gripping a prospective client's hand as if it were granite and theirs was a water balloon is a bad technique. Winning the fight of the too forceful handshake will not result in a sale. Rather, it may end up hurting the other person's hand and giving them an unfavorable opinion of you.

**Many people are sensitive** to others violating their personal space, whether they are standing too near or touching too much. Be careful that standing too near to someone or excessively touching them might be perceived as intrusive. However, pay attention to the other person's body language as well; what seems invasive to one person may appear pleasant to another.

**Not smiling;** smiling conveys warmth and energy, which might persuade a prospective customer that you are pleasant. When you don't smile, your facial expressions may appear uninviting or unapproachable.

**Avoiding direct eye contact**, when you avoid seeing someone in the eyes, it implies that you have something to conceal or that you can't be trusted. Your aim is to build trust and close the deal, so make eye contact whenever feasible to help your cause. According to research, maintaining eye contact between 60-70 percent of the time is best for building rapport. When people like or agree with you in a discussion, they immediately extend the amount of time they gaze into your eyes.

**Don't be a statue**; although fidgeting, slouching, or crossing your arms is undesirable, standing exactly straight and still can be scary. It's ideal to stand professionally yet naturally, so you seem at ease and the customer does as well. Try to adopt their stance.

**Hiding your hands**; some people strive to keep their hand movements to a minimum when speaking in order to appear more professional. However, communicating with your hands can help you communicate your point more effectively by reducing filler words and seeming reluctance. Also, displaying your palms while speaking conveys openness and honesty.

It is impossible to overstate the value of displaying positive body language in sales or any commercial transaction - it may make all the difference. Don't give the wrong message by damaging your own nonverbal communication. When you come into a meeting, be prepared and well-rehearsed. Be mindful of what you do while speaking as well. After all, you are giving visual accompaniment to your brilliant words. When your words and actions are in sync, you'll notice fewer closed doors and more closed deals. You are correct if you believe these things are obvious. Frequently, the things that consumers claim work best are the ones that salespeople overlook or take for granted.

## Things to concentrate on

**Maintain eye contact**; after presenting your prospect with two textual alternatives, you notice that his gaze is drawn to one of them more than the other. If you also notice his eyes widening or his pupils expand, you can be positive that he is more interested in this alternative. individuals who are drawn to individuals or items tend to glance at them for longer and more frequently. A person may strive to look indifferent, but his gaze will always return to the item that piques his attention the most. For many years, researchers have known that the size of a person's eye pupil is a crucial indicator of their emotional reactions. The pupils are a portion of our body over which we have little control. As a result, pupil dilation can be a very efficient method of determining someone's level of interest. Pupils dilate for a variety of reasons, including memory load and cognitive difficulties, but they also dilate to indicate pleasant thoughts about the person or thing we're talking to or looking at. When someone is less than responsive, his or her pupils constrict naturally.

**Take note of facial expressions**; someone who agrees with you will often grin and nod as you talk. Compressed or pursed lips, lowered brows, a tight mouth, clenched jaw muscles, or a head moved slightly aside, resulting in awkward sidelong eye contact, indicate disagreement.

**Learn what gestures mean**; in general, the more open your customer's arms are, the more open he or she will be to the sales process. Keep an eye out for expansive, inviting gestures that appear to flow freely. When someone reaches out to you or makes several open-hand motions, it is typically a show of curiosity and receptivity. People who feel defensive or furious, on the other hand, may fold their arms over their chests, clench their fists, or tightly hold their arms or wrists. Hand and arm movements are one of the strongest indications of emotional shifts as the negotiation develops. For instance, as you begin the conversation, the prospect's hands may be freely resting on the table. If they move away or hide beneath the table, it's a clue that something disturbing or undesirable has occurred. When someone is going to make a genuine revelation, they will generally reveal their hands, either by laying both hands on the table or by gesticulating while they talk.

**Concentrate on the shoulders and torso**; the shoulders and torso are significant in nonverbal communication. The more your customers/clients like and agree with you, the more they will lean toward you, or stand in front of or beside you. When you say or do anything they disagree with or are unsure about, they will tend to lean back and create more distance between the two of you. You've probably lost their interest if you notice them move their shoulders and body away from you. Orienting away from someone in this manner, regardless of the words uttered, nearly invariably implies detachment or disengagement. When individuals are engaged, they will turn to face you, "pointing" with their torso. However, if they are uncomfortable, they will look away, giving you "the cold shoulder." If someone is feeling defensive, they may try to protect their body with a pocketbook, briefcase, laptop, or other object. People who agree tend to mimic one other's actions. One will take the lead, while the other will follow. If you find your prospect has adopted the same fundamental body alignment as you, shift slightly and observe whether he follows suit. If he does, you know you've made a good impression.

**Read foot signals**; not only are our feet and legs our primary mode of mobility, but they are also the key markers of our "fight, flight, or freeze" survival techniques. They are also trained to react faster than the speed of cognition. The limbic brain system has already made sure that, depending on the scenario, our feet and legs are set to freeze in place, run away, or kick out in defense before we've had time to create any conscious strategy. If someone is seated with their ankles crossed and their legs stretched forward, they are usually feeling good about you. However, if you see your feet being pulled away from you, wrapped in a tight ankle lock, directed at the exit, or wrapped around the legs of a chair, you should suspect withdrawal and disengagement.

Finally, be watchful without being obtrusive. Trust your instincts, but increase your accuracy by deliberately evaluating the nonverbal cues conveyed. And keep in mind that you are already lot better at this than you realize. For the last several million years, successfully understanding body language has helped the human species thrive. The top salesmen have simply transformed a survival skill into a sophisticated sales tactic.

Key idea 7

# Sales isn't complete until payment for goods is made.

Payment processing is an important part of every organization since it influences customers happiness and total sales performance. In today's fast-paced digital environment, customers demand a smooth and speedy payment experience. Businesses may improve their clients experience and increase revenue by using effective payment processing solutions. We'll look at some helpful hints for organizations looking to improve their payment processing and increase revenue. To create a great client experience, a seamless and speedy payment procedure is required. When customers encounter issues or experience delays throughout the payment process, they may grow irritated and abandon their transaction. A smooth and hassle-free payment experience, on the other hand, may create a lasting impression on clients, leading to higher satisfaction and repeat purchases. Offering different payment alternatives is one of the most successful strategies to increase sales through payment processing. When it comes to making payments, various clients have varied preferences. Businesses may respond to a greater range of client preferences by offering a number of payment options such as credit cards, digital wallets, and internet banking. This adaptability improves the entire client experience and raises the chance of the purchase being completed. Many payment processors or fintech solution providers provide a full range of payment processing services, such as credit card processing, mobile payments, e-commerce solutions, and more. According to studies, businesses that provide different payment alternatives might see improved conversion rates and increased revenue. A poll found that 56% of respondents would abandon their shopping cart if their chosen payment option was not available. As a result, by providing different payment alternatives, businesses may minimize cart abandonment and increase revenues. Businesses may improve their payment processing skills and, as a result, increase their revenues by working with reputable payment processors.

**Optimize the Checkout Process**; Businesses must optimize the checkout process to offer a seamless and user-friendly consumer experience. A simplified and speedy checkout experience may minimize cart abandonment and raise conversion rates dramatically. Businesses should streamline the checkout process and reduce the amount of information necessary to optimize it. Implementing a guest checkout option allows clients to purchase without first creating an account, removing the need for time-consuming registration processes. Reducing the amount of form fields and just requesting necessary information will help to speed up the checkout process. Using auto-fill tools and offering clear instructions can improve the user experience even further. Customers may be guided through each stage by progress indicators, which keep them informed of progress and remaining steps.

Furthermore, adding renowned payment channels helps boost client confidence.

During the checkout process, displaying security badges and SSL certifications helps convince customers that their financial information is secure.

**Ensure Secure Payment Transactions;** organizations must ensure secure payment transactions to protect client data and develop confidence. Because online transactions are becoming more common, it is critical to adopt strong security measures throughout the payment process. Adherence to industry standards such as Payment Card Industry Data Security Standard (PCI DSS) compliance is an important step in safeguarding payment transactions. PCI DSS establishes rules and regulations for managing credit card information securely. Businesses may reduce the risk of data breaches and unauthorized access to sensitive consumer data by adhering to these guidelines.

Another critical part of safeguarding financial transactions is the use of encryption methods. When using Secure Sockets Layer (SSL) or Transport Layer Security (TLS) protocols, client data is encrypted during transmission, making it impossible for hackers to intercept and decrypt the data.

**Businesses should also invest in strong authentication procedures**. Using multi-factor authentication adds a layer of protection by forcing consumers to give additional verification, such as a one-time password or fingerprint scan, in addition to their payment credentials. Display trusted security provider trust seals and logos prominently on your website to reassure clients about the security safeguards in place. Businesses that prioritize security may create trust in their clients and improve their propensity to buy.

**Leverage on Mobile Payment Solutions;** in today's digital world, companies must rely on mobile payment solutions. Offering mobile payment alternatives, with the increasing usage of smartphones, may considerably improve the ease and accessibility of making purchases. Customers may make purchases using their cellphones utilizing mobile payment systems, removing the need for actual credit cards or cash. Customers may securely save their payment information on their smartphones and complete transactions with a few taps using popular mobile payment platforms such as Apple Pay, Google Pay, and Samsung Pay. Businesses may tap into the rising number of customers who want to make purchases using their smartphones by incorporating mobile payment solutions into their payment processing procedures. This accessibility has the potential to improve revenue and broaden client reach.

**Implement Automated repeating Billing;** automated repeating billing is a beneficial sales tactic, especially for firms that provide subscription-based products or services. Businesses may expedite the payment process for clients who choose recurring payments by utilizing automated recurring billing systems. Clients no longer need to manually begin payments each billing cycle, with automatic recurring billing. This ease of use minimizes friction and assures on-time payments, resulting in increased business cash flow and lower churn rates.

## Provide Early Payment Incentives

Encouraging clients to pay early may be extremely beneficial to businesses. Businesses may promote quick payments and enhance their cash flow by giving incentives such as discounts or exclusive offers to clients who pay before the due date. Early payment incentives provide value to clients and generate a feeling of urgency, motivating them to make their payments sooner rather than later. By assuring timely income creation, this method may help organizations maintain a healthy financial position and increase sales.

and experience. Effective salespeople frequently develop industry-specific skills, knowledge, and habits. The factors that make "The Money Bag Salesman," as discussed in this book, may help any salesperson create deeper relationships with potential clients, close more sales, and ultimately increase a company's income. Learning about "The Money Bag Salesman's" talents and qualities will help you understand your professional strengths and find areas for growth in your sales.

# Final Summary

There is no one technique to become a successful salesperson, but the behaviors listed above are critical to giving your clients a favorable sales experience. You're already on your way to being "The Money Bag Salesman" if you can manage a "no," be honest, and sensitive, minimize ambiguity, make your client feel like family, and make payment methods and terms very easy for the clients. A sales job can offer competitive income, a flexible work environment, and opportunities for professional advancement. To reap these rewards, a salesman must establish trusted connections with their clients to accomplish or surpass their sales targets.

A competent salesperson nowadays possesses a distinct set of talents, instincts,